Tan Kuo

Caribbean Supper Club
Recipe Book
2nd Edition

 By Monica Cudjoe & Karie-Ann Lee Sylvester

This 2nd edition is published in 2021 by Tan Rosie Foods Ltd
Tan Rosie Foods Ltd
Unit 4 Chancel Way Industrial Estate
Chancel Way
Witton
Birmingham
B6 7AU United Kingdom
© Copyright 2021 text, photography and design: Karie-Ann Lee
Sylvester & Monica Cudjoe, Tan Rosie Foods Ltd www.tanrosie.com
email: info@tanrosie.com

ISBN 978-0-9572771-4-4

First published in 2012 by Tan Rosie Foods Ltd
© Copyright 2012

Social Media:
Twitter: @tanrosie
Instagram: @tanrosiefoods
Facebook: /tanrosie
YouTube: Tan Rosie

You can buy this book directly from the publisher at www.tanro-
sie.com
It's also available to download in ebook format from Apple Books on
the iTunes Store or Amazon.com

Contents

This recipe book is dedicated to the memory of Priscilla Rosanna "Tan Rosie" Cudjoe, from Carriacou, Grenada.
Beloved mother, tanty, grandmother and great grandmother.

Introduction

Whilst growing up in Carriacou, Grenada, I have always had a fascination with cooking especially with the abundance of fresh fruit, vegetables and fish that surrounded me in the Caribbean.

Food is something which has always brought my family together through big celebrations to small family gatherings.

Since my children were young, we have always had a big family and friends barbeque at my home. These are fantastic occasions where everyone can meet, chat, reminisce and most importantly eat great Caribbean food!

Since starting up our business in 2010, my daughter Lee and I discovered the idea of 'Supper Clubs' and decided to give it a whirl. Supper clubs started off in Cuba they're called "Paladres" whereby local house wives open up their homes for paying guests to eat their traditional home cooked meals.

Supper Clubs are popping up all around the UK and it's a great way to eat great food by 'home cooks.' It's also a brilliant way to meet and chat to like-minded 'foodies' in a friendly relaxed environment.

Our first supper club evening in 2011 was based around the culinary delights of my home country Grenada. We thought it would be a great idea to offer our guests a chance to sample some of the dishes that I grew up with as a child. The response was phenomenal! We have had an amazing set of guests dining in our living room and we've made some great friends in the process.

All of our supper club recipes are authentic Caribbean dishes, many of which have my own unique twist. They are very easy to follow and very tasty.

Caribbean cuisine is a fusion of many cultures such as African, English, French, Dutch, Indian, Spanish and Chinese. Contrary to popular belief, Caribbean food is not all 'hot.' We use chillies, namely 'scotch bonnet peppers' where necessary and in different amounts. We use a mixture of hot (scotch bonnet pepper) and sweet spices such as cinnamon, nutmeg (native to Grenada) and allspice (pimento).

There are common dishes that are eaten in most Caribbean islands such as, rice and peas, coo coo (polenta) and curry goat, but each island has it's own unique regional difference which makes Caribbean cuisine extremely varied and exciting.

Monica Cudjoe, Tan Rosie Foods

Appetizers

Corn Fritters

These delicious Corn Fritters are a typical dish that has been cooked within my family kitchen back in Carriacou, Grenada since I can remember. It's a great way to use up fresh corn on the cob and it makes a great tasting snack.

Makes 24

Ingredients:

4 Fresh Sweet Corn Cobs or 1 Tin of Sweet Corn
4 Spring Onions chopped
1 Red Chilli chopped
1 Green Chilli chopped
1 tsp Salt
1 tsp Black Pepper
1 Beaten Egg
1 Cup Plain flour or Channa Flour
1tsp Baking Powder
Cooking Oil for deep frying
1 tbsp Fresh Coriander chopped
Water or Milk to combine

Method:

1. Remove Corn from cob using a sharp knife and place in a mixing bowl.
2. Add all other ingredients (except water/milk) to corn.
3. Mix all ingredients together
4. Blend in water/milk and mix to a "dropping or sticky" consistency.
5. Let mixture rest for 10/15 minutes
6. Heat oil in deep fryer or shallow fry in a saucepan and drop spoonfuls of the mixture into the hot oil and fry until golden brown.
7. Remove from the oil with a slotted spoon and place on absorbent paper towels.
8. Serve with a dipping sauce.

Tip: These can be made vegan by replacing the egg for an egg substitute and using nut milk or water to combine.

Plantain Crisps

Plantain crisps are a Caribbean classic. They are a great snack and can be made in advance and stored for eating at a later date. They taste great with a dipping sauce or with a dusting of sea salt.

Serves 12

Ingredients:
2-3 Green Plantains sliced thinly (a food processor using the slicing attachment is ideal or a mandolin).
Lime Juice or Lemon Juice
Salt
Oil for deep frying

Method:
1. Place sliced green plantain in a bowl and add a couple of pinches of salt, lemon or lime juice and a little water - mix and leave for 10-15 minutes.
2. Remove from bowl and dry well before deep frying.
3. Fry until crisp.
4. Turn out onto absorbent kitchen paper.
5. Serve with Pineapple & Mint Sauce (page 21).

Tips:
1. When crisps are cooked, they can be placed in an airtight container until ready. The container must be airtight or the crisps will be soft.
2. The crisps can be twice cooked to achieve a crispier texture.
3. You can also use Sweet Potatoes, Cassava or Yucca using the same method.

Appetizers

Accras (Salt Fish Fritters)

Accras or Salt Fish Fritters are a very common snack food in the Caribbean. If we are having a family party, we always have salt fish fritters on the menu. We eat these with a mild or hot chilli dip and they taste great with a salad as a starter. Try to eat them hot or warm, as the flavours taste better.

Makes 24

Ingredients:
8oz Salt Cod
1 Cup or 250g Plain Flour
1tsp Baking Powder
2 Eggs beaten
½ tsp Salt
½ tsp Black Pepper
1 tbsp Fish Sauce
1 Red Chilli minced
1 Green Chilli minced
4 Spring Onions finely chipped
1 tbsp Fresh Thyme leaves
Milk to combine

Method:
1. Soak salt cod overnight in cold water and juice of lemon and change water twice.
2. Next day, drain salt cod, pour over boiling water and let steep for 10-15 minutes - then drain.
3. Flake salt cod.
4. Combine all other ingredients in a bowl and mix well (the mixture can be blended in a food processor for a finer texture). The batter should be "dropping" consistency.
5. Heat oil in shallow frying pan to medium heat.
6. Drop spoonfuls of the mixture into the frying pan and cook until golden brown, turning occasionally.
7. Remove from heat with slotted spoon and place on a dish lined with absorbent kitchen paper.
8. Serve while still hot or warm

Pumpkin Bread Rolls

This savoury pumpkin bread is a fun way to eat this delicious vegetable. Pumpkins are a popular vegetable in the Caribbean. It's easy to make, it's got a beautiful colour and tastes amazing. **Makes 12**

Ingredients:
4 cups or 1kg Strong Bread Flour
2 cups or 500g Pumpkin, steamed and pureed and cooled
2 Tsp Yeast
100g Softened butter
2 Tsp Salt
1 Tbsp Sugar
500ml Warmed milk
Baking tray
Baking Parchment

Method:
1. In a mixing bowl combine all the dry ingredients.
2. Add butter and blend in.
3. Combine all the ingredients with milk to form a soft dough.
4. Knead on a floured surface for 5 minutes.
5. Return to bowl and cover with a damp clean tea towel and rest for 1 hour.
6. After 1 hour knock back the dough and knead again.
7. Divide into 12 equal portions and shape into balls.
8. Place dough balls onto a baking tray lined with baking parchment.
9. Cover and leave to rise for 45 minutes.
10. Preheat oven to gas mark 7
11. Place dough balls in oven and bake for 35 to 40 minutes until golden brown

Sauces

Sweet Chilli Sauce

This has been a firm favourite from our Supper Club events. It's a great dipping sauce that's perfect with fritters and crisps. It's also very quick and easy to make.

Ingredients:
1 Cup Sugar
½ Cup Rice Wine Vinegar
½ Cup Water
2 Red Chillies finely chopped
Chopped Fresh coriander

Method:
1. Place sugar, water and rice wine vinegar in a pan and slowly bring to the boil.
2. Reduce heat and simmer for 5 minutes until reduced down.
3. Add chopped chillies and cook for a further 5 minutes.
4. Remove from heat and add coriander.
5. Allow to cool and serve.

Spicy Banana Chutney

We love this banana chutney recipe. It's spicy and tasty and it's superb with curries or strong cheeses and a glass of red wine!

Ingredients:

1kg Ripe Bananas peeled and chopped
1 Scotch Bonnet Pepper, de seeded and finely chopped
2 Garlic Cloves
250g finely chopped Onions
500g Soft Brown Sugar
225g Finely grated Ginger
2tsp Allspice
1tsp Cinnamon
400mls Malt Vinegar
1tsp Salt

Method:

1. In a preserving pan, place vinegar, onions, garlic, ginger and pepper. Slowly bring to the boil, stirring occasionally.
2. When brought to boil, reduce heat and simmer gently until onions are soft.
3. Add sugar, bananas allspice, cinnamon and salt.
4. Simmer until sugar has dissolved.
5. Turn up heat to medium and stir frequently until mixture thickens.
6. Pour into sterilized jars and seal.

Sauces
Mixed Pepper Creole Sauce

We use this Creole sauce with Coo Coo (polenta) and Salt Fish. It's very traditional in the Caribbean to use this sauce with any kind of fish especially if it's fried. It's very easy and quick to make and tastes amazing.

Ingredients:
1 Red pepper cut in strips
1 Green Pepper cut into strips
1 Yellow Pepper cut into strips
1 Small red chilli chipped finely
2 Cloves garlic minced finely
1 small Red Onion
1 tsp Fresh thyme leaves
¼ Cup Olive Oil
Salt & Black Pepper to taste
¼ tsp Sugar
1oz Butter
250g diced tomato, deseeded and peeled

Method:
1. Place saucepan on medium heat.
2. Add oil and butter.
3. Add onion and sauté for 5 minutes until soft, stirring occasionally.
4. Add garlic and fry for 1 minute, stirring to prevent sticking.
5. Add peppers and cook for 5 minutes.
6. Add tomatoes, thyme, chilli, salt, pepper and sugar, stirring.
7. Cook for 5 minutes or until sauce reduces to a slightly thickish consistency.
8. Remove from heat and serve.

Chilli Lime Sauce

Another favourite of our Supper Club! Limes are used extensively in Carriacou, Grenada. They taste fantastic in this sauce recipe especially with a kick of chilli. You can use the sauce with fritters, crisps and burgers. Also, the sauce tastes great with BBQ chicken wings!

Ingredients:
1 Cup Sugar
3 Quarter Cup Water
Juice and grated zest of 3 Limes
1 Red Chilli finely chopped
1 tbsp Chopped fresh coriander
¼ Cup Rice Wine Vinegar

Method:
1. Place sugar, water, juice of lemon and rice wine vinegar into a saucepan and bring to boil.
2. Reduce heat and simmer for 5 Minutes
3. Add chopped chilli, zest of lemon and continue to simmer for 5 minutes.
4. Remove from heat and add chopped coriander and serve when cool.

Pineapple & Mint Sauce

The acidity of pineapple with mint, makes for a great sauce. You can use it with any kind of fried dishes from burgers, sausages to samosas.

Ingredients:
2 Cups Fresh Pineapple finely chopped
1 Cup Sugar
½ Cup Water
¼ Cup Rice Wine Vinegar
1 Cup Chopped fresh mint leaves
1 Red Chilli finely chopped
¼ tsp Salt
¼ tsp Black Pepper
2 tbsp Chopped fresh Coriander

Method:
1. In a saucepan place pineapple, sugar, chillies, salt, black pepper, water and rice wine vinegar and simmer for 5 minutes.
2. Remove pan from heat then add half the chopped mint and coriander then allow to cool.
3. Add remainder of mint when cool.

Mango Mojo Sauce

Mango Mojo is a traditional Cuban sauce. It can be used with a variety dishes to enhance any meal. We've used this sauce to accompany our Supper Club appetizers such as fritters and crisps, which always goes down well with our guests.

Ingredients:

2 Large mangoes peeled and chopped
8 Cloves of garlic finely minced
¼ Cup extra virgin olive oil
¼ Cup freshly squeezed lime juice
¼ Cup freshly squeezed orange juice
¼ tsp ground cumin
¼ tsp Cayenne Pepper
Salt & Black pepper to season

Method:

1. On a medium heat, place oil in saucepan add minced garlic and stir for about 30 seconds without burning - it is just to fragrant the oil.
2. Add lime juice, orange and combine by stirring.
3. Add cumin, salt, pepper, cayenne pepper and diced mango.
4. Bring to the boil and simmer gently for about 5 minutes stirring occasionally to prevent sticking.
5. Check for seasoning and cool for 5 minutes.
6. In a glass bowl pour sauce and let it rest covered.
7. Allow sauce to rest for 2-4 hours before serving. This allows flavours to blend well. The sauce should thicken on cooling.

Tip:

This sauce can be kept in the fridge for up to 1 week.

Sauces
Spiced Tomato Sauce

We've always made our own tomato sauce and it tastes so much better than a shop bought variety. Of course, if you'd like some heat add some finely chopped Scotch Bonnet Pepper to the mixture. We used this sauce with our Macaroni Pie (page 64) to add extra flavour to the dish.

Ingredients:
2 Cups Chopped Fresh Tomatoes, skinned (2 tins chopped tomatoes may be used)
1 Cup Finely chopped Onions
3 Cloves Garlic, minced
¼ Cup Olive Oil
50g Butter
1 tsp Sugar
¼ tsp Salt
1 Vegetable stock cube
1 tsp Dried Oregano
1 tsp Dried Thyme
1 tbsp Chopped Fresh Basil
1 tbsp Tomato puree
½ Cup Water

Method:
1. On medium heat, place saucepan with olive oil and butter to melt.
2. Add onions and sauté for 5 minutes, stirring occasionally.
3. Add garlic and chilli, then stir for 1 minute.
4. Add tomatoes, sugar, vegetable stock, dried herbs, water, salt and pepper.
5. Bring to the boil and simmer gently, stirring occasionally for 30 minutes.
6. Add tomato puree and basil.
7. Continue to simmer for a further 5-10 minutes.
8. Adjust seasoning to taste.

Tip:
The sauce should be of a thick consistency. To obtain a smooth sauce, blend with a stick blender until smooth.

Starters

Salt Fish Fried Patties

Salt fish is such a common fish used in Caribbean culture. Here, we've combined dumplings with the salt fish mixture to form a patty. It's the perfect snack food that your family and friends will enjoy.

Makes 6/8

Ingredients for Salt Fish:

8oz Salted Cod
1 Large Onion finely chopped
1 Garlic Clove finely minced
1 tbsp Fresh thyme chopped
50g Butter
30mls Olive Oil
3 Tomatoes peeled de seeded and chopped
1 Red pepper sliced
1 Yellow pepper sliced
1 Green pepper sliced
Salt & Black pepper
1 Scotch Bonnet Pepper

Dumplings Ingredients:

See Ackee & Salt Fish with Fried Dumpling Recipe page 32

Method:

1. Soak salt cod in cold water overnight, changing the water twice to remove excess salt.
2. Soak salt cod in boiling water for 1 hour.
3. Remove from water.
4. Remove skin, bones and flake cod fish.
5. In saucepan place oil and butter.
6. Place chopped onions in a pan and sauté for 5-10 minutes without colouring.
7. Add minced garlic and continue to sauté for 1 minute without browning, add peppers and cook for 5 minutes.
8. Add salt fish and whole scotch bonnet pepper and continue to cook through for approximately 3-5 minutes.
9. Season to taste with salt and pepper and remove scotch bonnet pepper.

Dumpling Method:

See Ackee & Salt Fish with Fried Dumpling Recipe page 32.

Patty Method:

1. Make 8 portions of dough on a floured surface.
2. Form into round balls, then roll out into discs. Roughly 20cm diameter forming half discs.
3. Place a teaspoon of salt fish mixture into the centre of the disc. Then, around one half of the disc, brush with water. Carefully bring the edges together and seal to form patty shape. Continue the same process until all patties are formed.
4. Deep fry in vegetable oil at 180oC for 2/3 minutes until golden brown. Serve with a tasty dip!

Pure de Calabaza
(Creamy Pumpkin Soup)

This is a great Cuban style pumpkin soup recipe which we had on our menu for our Cuban Supper Club night. It went down a storm with our guests! The colour looks amazing and it tastes great too. Serve with some warm bread rolls.

Serves 6

Ingredients:

2 tbsp Olive oil
1 Large onion finely chopped
3 Garlic Cloves minced
1kg Pumpkin peeled, de seeded and cut into cubes
1 Small scotch bonnet pepper de seeded and finely chopped
4 Cups vegetable stock
1 Cup single cream
Salt & Black pepper to taste
Chopped chives for decoration (optional)

Method:

1. In a large saucepan, place olive oil and bring to heat.
2. Add onions and sauté for 5 minutes without colouring.
3. Add garlic and scotch bonnet pepper and continue to sauté for 1 minute.
4. Add pumpkin and vegetable stock, bring to the boil then reduce heat and simmer for 30 minutes until pumpkin is tender.
5. Using a stick blender, place mixture into a jug and blend until smooth.
6. Return soup mixture to saucepan, add cream, salt and black pepper to taste.
7. Reheat and serve in warmed bowls, with a swirl of cream and chopped chives as decoration.

Balchi di Pisca
(Salt Cod Balls)

Salt cod balls are a very popular dish in Aruba. We had this dish as a starter for our Aruban supper club night, which was served with a chutney. It's great with a hot sauce dip too.

Makes 24

Ingredients:

8oz Salt cod soaked overnight in cold water and discard
3 Medium potatoes peeled and diced
1 Large tomato peeled and chopped
1 Medium onion finely chopped
1 Garlic clove minced
1 tsp **Tan Rosie's Garlic & pepper Sauce (HOT)**
1 Cup plain flour
½ tsp Freshly grated nutmeg
Salt & Black Pepper
1 Egg beaten
1 tbsp Fish sauce
½ Green pepper chopped

Method:

1. Immerse pre-soaked salt cod in boiling water for 15 minutes.
2. Remove bones and skin from fish and flake.
3. Cook potatoes until tender.
4. Drain the potatoes and mash together with flaked fish until well combined.
5. In a food processor, place tomato, green peppers, onion, garlic, hot sauce, nutmeg, flour and salt and black pepper, 1 tbsp fish sauce and blend for a few seconds.
6. Pour sauce over mashed cod and potato mixture and combine all ingredients well.
7. Add beaten egg and mix together. The mixture should be firm enough to form balls about the size of a walnut.
8. Fry balls in hot deep fat until golden brown.

Tip:

Smoked salmon or smoked haddock can be substituted for salt cod.

Spiced BBQ Hake

Fish is a staple ingredient in the Caribbean and it can be cooked so simply to create tremendous flavour. Fish is always a good starter dish option and here we've BBQ'd it with a simple marinade. Try it

Serves 4

Ingredients:
8 Hake steaks sliced 1" thick
1 Whole Lime
Juice from 1 Lime
1 Scotch Bonnet Pepper
1 Tsp Salt
1 Tsp Black Pepper
1 Tbsp Parsley, finely chopped
3 Tbsp Olive Oil
3 Tbsp White Wine Vinegar

Method:
1. In a bowl place the lime juice, olive oil, salt, black pepper, vinegar and parsley, then mix together.
2. Chop a little of the scotch bonnet pepper skin finely and mix into the bowl.
3. Place your fish in a bowl and pour over marinade. Leave for 2 hours in the fridge.
4. Cook on the bbq and serve with a salad. Slice the 2nd lime and drizzle some of the juice to serve. Simply delicious!

Tip:
Any meaty fish can be used such as salmon, monkfish or red snapper.

Ackee & Salt Fish
with Fried Dumplings

Ackee and Salt Fish is a very famous and traditional Jamaican dish. It's a great crowd-pleaser, very colourful and tastes fantastic.

Serves 6

Ackee Ingredients:
450g Salt cod
1 Lemon
1oz Butter
2 tbsp Olive oil
1 Onion minced
2 Garlic cloves minced
8oz Tomatoes skinned & chopped
1 Small scotch bonnet pepper, de seeded and chopped
1 tbsp Freshly chopped thyme
4 Spring onions chopped
¼ tsp Black pepper
1 Can Ackee, drained

Dumplings Ingredients:
2 Cups Self raising flour
1tsp Salt
1oz Butter
Water to make firm dough
Oil for frying
2 Tsp Sugar

Method:
1. Place cod in a bowl of cold water in juice of lemon and soak for 24 hours. Change water & lemon 2-3 times to remove saltiness.
2. After 24 hours, remove and drain water. Place in a bowl, add boiling water and leave to steep for 15 minutes.
3. Drain, remove, skin and de-bone the fish, then flake.
4. In a saucepan, place oil and butter on a medium heat, gently sauté onions and garlic for 5 minutes without browning.
5. Add tomatoes, scotch bonnet peppers and continue to sauté for 3-5 minutes.
6. Add salt fish, thyme, spring onions and simmer for 5 minutes and adjust seasoning.
7. Add drained ackee and allow this to warm through, but not boil. Then serve with fried dumplings.

Dumplings Method:
1. Place the flour, salt, sugar and butter into a bowl and rub the butter to form breadcrumbs. Mix to a film dough with warm water. Then leave to rest for 15/20 minutes.
2. Form into small balls, place oil in a frying pan and bring up to medium heat
3. Add dumplings and fry until golden brown and cooked through, turning as required to prevent burning.
4. When cooked, remove and drain and serve with salt fish and ackee.

Tip:
You can make the dumplings flat, which puff up when fried and produce an air pocket to stuff with salt fish, bacon etc. Simply roll out into a disc and fry. Making them flat speeds up the cooking process and ensures the centre is cooked through.

Mains

Grenadian Stewed Chicken

Stewed or Stew Chicken, is a classic dish made in many family homes across Grenada and the many parts of the Caribbean. It uses a particular technique called 'browning' or 'sugaring,' which involves caramalising sugar to fry off the meat. This dish has a wonderful aroma and tastes delicious too.

Serves 4

Ingredients for chicken:

8 Chicken thighs, deboned & diced
1 Tsp Ground Allspice
½ Tsp Ground Clove
½ Tsp Ground Nutmeg
1 Tbsp Fresh Thyme
3 Cloves Garlic, minced
2" piece Fresh Root Ginger grated
1 Onion, finely chopped
1 Tbsp Soya Sauce
1 Tbsp Worcestershire Sauce
1 Tsp Ground Black Pepper
1½ Tsp Sea Salt
1 Tbsp Olive Oil

Ingredients for Stew:

1 Tbsp Olive Oil
1 Tbsp White Sugar
200ml Chicken Stock
1 Whole Scotch Bonnet Pepper
1 Small Green Pepper, diced
1 Small Red Pepper, diced
1 Small Yellow Pepper, diced

Method:

1. In a mixing bowl, combine chicken and the other chicken ingredients together, coating all of the meat.
2. Cover bowl with the seasoned chicken and leave in the fridge for at least 2 hours or overnight.
3. Place a saucepan onto a medium heat, add some oil and heat through. Add the sugar and caramelise or brown, to a medium colour (not too dark). This is what gives the dish that lovely rich, brown colour.
4. Add some oil to a saucepan, add chicken pieces, leaving aside the seasoning ingredients for the time being and fry/seal the meat.
5. Continue stirring chicken to allow an all over coating with browning liquid.
6. Stir and cook for about 5 minutes.
7. Next add the other seasoning ingredients and cook for a further 5 minutes.
8. Add the whole scotch bonnet pepper and chicken stock and bell peppers bring to the boil, then reduce the heat and simmer or place in an oven dish for 15 minutes.
9. After 15 minutes, seperate the chicken from the sauce and set aside in a separate bowl, then add the diced bell peppers and stir. Reduce the sauce for a further 10 minutes on a high heat until it's thickened.
10. Add the chicken back into the pot and mix through. Then, remove from the heat and adjust seasoning if needed. Serve with rice and peas or plain boiled rice.

Tip:

You can make this dish without the red, yellow and green peppers if you prefer. It's more tradtional and

Mains
Curry Mutton

Curry mutton is one of our favourite dishes from the Caribbean. We always have this dish at family parties and get togethers of all kinds. Usually at parties, this is served towards the end of the night with roti, plain rice or rice and peas.

Serves 4

Ingredients:

1 kg Mutton diced with any gristle and fat removed
1 Large onion chopped
3 Cloves Garlic minced
2 tbsp Curry Powder
Few sprigs fresh Thyme
2 Bay leaves
1 tsp Ground allspice
½ tsp Ground cloves
Vegetable Oil for frying
Knob Butter for frying
1 Scotch bonnet pepper left whole
2 Cups or 500ml vegetable stock, lamb stock or water
1 Cup or 250ml Coconut milk
1 tsp Salt
1 tsp Black Pepper

Method:

1. Place the mutton, curry powder, allspice, cloves, bay leaves and oil in a bowl.
2. Mix all ingredients together well. Cover bowl and marinade for 2 to 3 hours or overnight in fridge.
3. In large frying pan place butter with a little oil, allow to melt on medium heat.
4. Fry off onions for a few minutes until softened. Add garlic and thyme and fry for a minute.
5. Add mutton to frying pan and fry on medium heat for about 10 to 15 minutes stirring frequently until brown.
6. Add stock, coconut milk and scotch bonnet pepper, bring to the boil.
7. Transfer to an oven dish with a lid and cook on a medium heat at 180 or gas mark 5/6 for 1 ½ hours.
8. After 1 ½ hours, stir. Check meat has cooked. Then put back into the oven with lid off for a further 15/20 mins to ensure sauce thickens.
8. Serve with Roti, boiled rice or rice and peas.

Tip:

1. Lamb, goat, chicken or beef can be used instead of mutton in this recipe.
2. A slow cooker can be used instead of the oven.

Pollo Borracho
(Drunken Chicken)

Pollo Borracho is a typical Cuban supper dish. Spanish olives, white wine and white rum are combined to create a great tasting chicken dish. Serve with saffron rice for an authentic Cuban meal.

Serves 6

Ingredients:

12 Chicken thighs skin removed
4 Cloves garlic minced
1 Large onion medium sliced
2 Bay leaves
1 Cup dry white wine
½ Cup white rum
1 Cup unpitted large green olives, drained
¼ Cup Spanish olive oil
1 tsp dried oregano
Sea salt and freshly ground black pepper to taste
Juice of 1 lime or lemon

Method:

1. With the juice of lemon or lime, wash chicken thighs. Pat dry using kitchen paper towels.
2. Place chicken in bowl. Massage salt, pepper and oregano into chicken thighs. Leave to marinade for 3 hours or overnight in the fridge.
3. In large heavy bottomed frying pan, heat olive oil over medium heat. Brown chicken thighs on either side, a light brown colour should be aimed for.
4. Remove browned chicken thighs from pan and set aside.
5. Reduce heat under pan to low add onions and garlic, cook until tender without colouring. This should take about 8 to 10 minutes.
6. Add bay leaves, wine, rum and olives bring to the boil.
7. Return chicken thighs to pan, cover and cook for 45 to 50 minutes.
8. Remove bay leaves. Serve with saffron rice.

Breadfruit Oildown

Oildown is Grenada's national dish . It's essentially a 1-pot dish with salted or preserved meats and a variety of vegetables. It's very easy to prepare and delicious to eat!

Serves 6

Ingredients:
½ lb smoked ham or gammon diced
1 tbsp olive oil
1 Large onion chopped
2 Cloves garlic minced
1 Red pepper diced
½ Scotch bonnet pepper de seeded, and stem removed and finely chopped
1 Bunch spring onions chopped
1 tbsp fresh thyme
4 Cups coconut milk
500g Spinach or callaloo chopped
1 Large breadfruit peeled and cut into 2" pieces
Sea salt and black pepper to taste
50g butter

Method:
1. Heat oil in a saucepan, sauté onions, for 5 minutes until soft.
2. Add peppers, garlic, spring onions, ham and thyme continue to sauté for a further 5 minutes, stirring at times
3. Add coconut milk and breadfruit and bring to the boil.
4. Reduce heat and simmer 30 minutes.
5. Add spinach and butter allow to wilt down for 5 minutes
6. Add salt and pepper to taste.

Jerk Belly Pork

Jerk is a traditional seasoning from Jamaica. It's delicious with chicken and especially pork. Belly pork is a wonderful cut of meat that can really handle the jerk flavours.

Serves 4 - 6

Ingredients for Jerk Seasoning:
See Tan Rosie's Jerk Chicken page 52

1kg Belly Pork cut into 1" slices

Method:
1. Place the pork into a bowl and pour over the marinade.
2. Cover and leave in the fridge to marinade overnight or for at least 2 hours.
3. Place in an oven dish and cook on a medium heat for 1 ½ hours covered.
4. After 1 ½ hours remove the cover, baste and put back in the oven for a further 15/20 mins uncovered until cooked.
5. Once cooked the pork should be succulent with crisp edges.
6. Serve with rice and peas or fried dumplings.

Yummy!

Bajan Beef Stew

We served this classic Barbadian (Bajan) stew with coconut rice on our Bajan supper club night. The beef was very tender and juicy with a rich sauce and complimented the coconut rice (page 74). You can also eat this dish with your favourite chutney for extra pizzazz!

Serves 6 - 8

Ingredients:

2 lbs beef, cubed
1 Large onion finely chopped
4 Garlic cloves finely minced
1 tbsp olive oil
1 tbsp Butter
½ tsp ground allspice
½ tsp ground cloves
1 tsp **Tan Rosie's Garlic & Pepper Sauce (HOT)**
or 1 Chilli Pepper
2 Sticks celery diced
½ lb carrots diced
1 tsp Fresh thyme
1 Bay leaf
½ tsp Dried oregano
1 Large beetroot diced
4 Cups beef stock/ vegetable stock
Salt and ground black pepper to taste
1 tsp Worcestershire sauce
1 tsp gravy browning
1 tbsp Butter and flour mixed to a paste
1 Beef stock cude

Method:

1. Place beef in bowl with onions, garlic, pepper sauce, allspice, cloves, herbs, Worcestershire sauce, celery and beef cubes.
2. Mix well and leave to marinate for at least 3 hours or overnight in the fridge.
3. In a frying pan place oil, bring to heat add oil and sauté marinated beef for about 10 minutes, turning to brown evenly.
4. Add stock and gravy browning and bay leaf bring to the boil.
5. Reduce heat and simmer on low heat for 1 hour or until beef is tender.
6. Add flour and butter paste to beef stew to thicken. Continue to stir until blended.
7. Add vegetables salt and pepper to taste, continue to cook until vegetables are tender for about 15 to 20 minutes.

Tip:

1. Stew can be cooked in a covered casserole dish in oven on medium heat for 1 ½ hours. For the last ½ hour of cooking place casserole on hob to reduce sauce to a thick consistency.
2. A slow cooker can also be used.

Mains
Spicy Slow Roast Mutton

Slow roasted meats are a common favourite in our home and this recipe is no exception. Caribbean spices such as allspice and cloves really make mutton come alive.

Serves 8 - 10

Ingredients:

1 Shoulder or leg of Mutton
2 Onions chopped
4 Cloves garlic
3 Scotch bonnet peppers de seeded and chopped
1 tbsp fresh thyme
½ Cup or 125g brown sugar
1 Bunch spring onions chopped
1 tsp ground allspice
1 tsp ground cloves
1 tsp freshly grated nutmeg
¼ Cup or 2 tbsp soya sauce
¼ Cup or 2 tbsp olive oil
1 tsp sea salt
Juice of 2 limes or lemons

Method:

1. In large bowl place mutton. Make some slashes in meat.
2. Place all other ingredients in food processor and blend together.
3. Rub marinade into meat, ensuring all marinade gets well into slashed areas and leave to marinade for up to 48 hours in the fridge.
4. Remove from fridge and leave to reach room temperature.
5. Preheat oven to high.
6. Place mutton in roasting pan, covered with foil roast for 20 minutes on high.
7. Reduce heat low and slow roast for 6 hours until meat is falling off bone.
8. For the last 45 minutes remove foil covering and baste meat with pan juices.
9. Remove from heat/oven and leave to rest, covered before pulling apart and serving.

Rice & Peas Chicken Pelau

This is another traditional dish from Carriacou, Grenada that's got my own twist. It's a very hearty meal and has been enjoyed by my family and friends for many years.

Serves 4

Ingredients:

250gm Long Grain Rice
40gm **'Tan Rosie's Jerk Rub'** or any other chicken seasoning
250g Pigeon Peas (or tinned variety) soaked overnight
4 Chicken thighs (skinned)
1 Medium Onion (minced)
2 Garlic cloves (diced)
1 Tin Coconut Milk
100gm Smoked Bacon or Salt Pork/Beef
1 Scotch Bonnet Pepper
Black Pepper to taste
2 tsp Fresh Thyme
2 tsp Vegetable Stock
500ml Water
Salad Leaves for serving

Method:

1. Massage Jerk Rub into chicken and leave overnight in fridge.
2. Heat oil in a pan, add chicken then brown.
3. Add bacon, onions & cook for 5mins.
4. Add coconut milk, peas, thyme, water, scotch bonnet pepper, stock and bring to boil, then simmer for 15mins on low heat.
5. Add rice and stir, bring to boil, cover and simmer for 15mins on low heat, then serve with a fresh salad.

Tip:

1. Make sure you remove scotch bonnet pepper before serving!
2. If using dried peas, soak overnight and cook to tender for 40 minutes.

Coo Coo & Baked Goat Fish

Coo Coo (polenta), is another traditional dish from Carriacou, Grenada that's got my own twist. It's a very hearty meal and has been enjoyed by my family and friends for many years.

Serves 6

Coo Coo Ingredients:
200gm Polenta/Corn Meal
1 ltr Water
30ml Olive Oil and Butter
1 tbsp Salt or Vegetable stock powder
Black Pepper to taste
3 Spring Onions
1 Tin coconut milk

Okra Ingredients:
250gm Okras (sliced)
Salt & Black Pepper to taste
250ml Water
1 sml Spring Onion (diced)

Goat Fish Ingredients:
3 Goat Fishes
1 tbsp Tan Rosie's Garlic & Pepper Sauce (HOT)
1 tbsp Fish Sauce
½ Lemon (Juice)
Salt & Black Pepper to taste
1 tbsp Fresh Thyme

Coo Coo method:
1. Add oil, butter and spring onions in pan then sauté for 1 minute.
2. Add water, coconut milk, vegetable stock and bring to boil.
3. Whisk polenta into boiling liquid until thick paste (if too thick add water) then cook for 5 minutes.
4. Butter a dish then pour into bowl.

Okra method:
1. Remove head & tail of okra.
2. Add oil to pan, add onions and fry for 5 minutes until softened.
3. Add okras, quartered tomatoes, water, salt & pepper.
4. Bring to boil and simmer for 10mins, then serve.

Goat Fish method:
1. Clean & gut fish.
2. Add to slashes to either side of fish.
3. Place all other ingredients into a bowl with fish and leave to marinade for ½ hour.
4. Remove fish, then shallow fry for 5 mins either side.
5. Then place in baking dish, cover then bake for 5 minutes on medium heat, then serve.

Tip:
1. Always whisk the polenta, as this prevents lumps occurring.
2. You can also use salmon or haddock as an alternative to Goat fish.

Mains
Chicken Roti

Chicken Roti is a fantastic street food dish served in many parts of the Caribbean. I've used a Paratha roti recipe which originates from India via Trinidad. It's great for lunch when you are at Paradise beach in Hillsborough town, Carriacou!

Serves 6

Chicken Curry Ingredients:

500gm Boned Chicken Thighs (Cubed).
40gm **'Tan Rosie Caribbean Style Curry Powder'**
1 tbsp Vegetable Oil
1 Scotch Bonnet Pepper
1 medium Potato (Cubed)
200ml Coconut Milk
1 Large Onion (Minced)
2 Garlic Cloves (Minced)
1 tsp Salt & Black Pepper
100 ml Water

Roti Ingredients:

500gm Flour
1 tbsp Baking Powder
1 tsp Salt
50gm Ghee
Water (enough to form soft dough)

To make the Chicken Curry:

1. Cut boned chicken thigh into cubes.
2. Massage curry powder into chicken & leave overnight.
3. Heat oil in a pan, then add onions & sauté for 5 mins until golden brown.
4. Add minced garlic & sauté for 1 minute.
5. Add seasoned chicken and fry until brown.
6. Add coconut milk, water, potato, salt, pepper & scotch bonnet pepper and cover pot and bring to boil & simmer for 40 mins.
7. Remove cover and reduce liquid until thickened.
8. Remove scotch bonnet pepper and serve.

To Make Roti:

1. Add flour, salt & baking powder into a bowl.
2. Add some water (enough to form a soft pliable dough) then mix for 5 mins.
3. Turn out onto floured surface & knead until smooth – cover & leave for 15mins.
4. Melt ghee in pan and add some flour to make a paste, then cut dough into 4 portions and make round balls and roll out into 10" disc.
5. Brush ghee paste onto disc and cut from centre of disc to outer edge and roll together to form a cone shape.
6. Place the cone on surface, push the peak down so it is flat and roll out into 12" diameter disc (the cone shape makes the layers).
7. Place on a hot tawa or gridle stone and cook for 1 min – turn and brush with ghee and repeat until brown specs appear.
9. Remove and cover with warm towel – then repeat until all the dough is cooked.

Tip:
Make sure you have a plate and warm towel ready for the rotis. Plus, it's important to leave the chicken to marinade for at least 2 hours or overnight.

Tan Rosie's Jerk Chicken

Jerk is a seasoning which originates from Jamaica. It's traditionally cooked on a BBQ with pimento wood, then chopped up and served with a jerk sauce or gravy. Try making this jerk marinade from scratch with this tasty recipe. If you need more heat, simply add a little more scotch bonnet pepper. Try cooking the jerk chicken on the BBQ for an even tastier flavour in the summer months!

Serves 4/6

Ingredients:

4 Spring Onions
1 Tbsp Fresh Thyme
1 Tsp Salt
2 Tsp Ground Allspice
1 Tsp Ground Nutmeg
1 Tsp Ground Cinnamon
1 Scotch Bonnet Pepper
2 Tsp Black Pepper
½ Cup or 125ml Soy Sauce
½ Cup or 125ml Olive Oil
¼ Cup or 2 Tbsp White Wine Vinegar
½ Cup or 125ml Orange Juice
1 Tbsp Fresh Grated Root Ginger
3 Cloves Garlic
1 Tbsp Worcestershire

2kg Chicken Thighs

Method:

1. Place all ingredients into a food processor and blend into a paste.
2. Cover the chicken with the marinade and leave in the fridge overnight or for 2 hours.
3. Preheat the oven to 230c or gas mark 8.
4. Place marinated chicken in an oven dish and cover with foil or lid. If you have skinned chicken, place skin side down and cook for 35 minutes.
5. After 35 minutes, turn over and baste chicken pieces and pace back in the oven with the lid off. This ensures the liquid is thickened and the chicken achieves a lovely roasted colour.
6. Serve with rice and peas and fresh greens.

Tip:

1. Use as much or as little of the scotch bonnet pepper as you require. Sometimes we only use a small section of the skin to add a little heat.
2. This marinade recipe will make more than you'll need for this amount of meat, so you can keep the excess in fridge or portion it out and freeze it for future use.

Vegetarian Dishes

Vegetarian Dishes
Aubergine, Chickpea & Sweet Potato Curry

You won't miss meat with our yummy veggie curry. It's easy to make, filling and delicious.

Serves 4

Ingredients:

1 kg Sweet Potato (white or orange) cut into 2" cubes
1 Tin Chickpeas, drained
500g Baby Aubergines, cut into 2" pieces
2 Tbsp Olive Oil for roasting vegetables
1 Tsp Salt
½ tsp Black Pepper
1 Large Onion, finely chopped
2 Garlic cloves
1 Whole Scotch Bonnet Pepper
2 Tsp Fresh Thyme
2" Piece Root Ginger, grated
2 Tbsp **Tan Rosie's Caribbean Style Curry Powder** or a mild curry powder
1 Tbsp Olive Oil
1 Tbsp Butter
1 Tin Coconut Milk
400ml Vegetable Stock
1 Tsp Sugar
Salt & Pepper to season
Knob of butter (optional)

Method:

1. Preheat the oven to gas mark 6 or 200oC.
2. In a roasting tray, place the sweet potato and aubergine, salt, and black pepper, then toss in the olive oil. Roast for 30 minutes.
3. Place a saucepan on a medium heat, add olive oil, butter and chopped onions and cook for 5 minutes until golden brown. Add garlic and ginger and sauté for a further 1 minute.
4. Add curry powder and fry for 1 minute.
5. Add coconut milk, vegetable stock, thyme, whole scotch bonnet pepper and sugar. Bring to the boil and simmer uncovered for 10 minutes to reduce down slightly.
6. Toss in roasted vegetables and chickpeas, then continue to cook for a further 5 minutes.
7. Adjust the seasoning if needed, remove scotch bonnet and discard.
8. Serve with basmati rice or roti.

Tip:

We have used the white sweet potato, as we find it has a better flavour and is less watery than the orange variety. It has a red skin and can be found at Asian supermarkets.

Vegetarian Dishes
Frijoles Negros & Bonito Bake
(Black Bean & Sweet Potato Bake)

Black Beans are used widely in Cuban food. This is a great recipe we came up with to utilize this tasty pulse. It's very comforting and moreish, so enjoy!

Serves 6

Ingredients For Black Bean Base/Stew:

2 Cups black beans cooked,
1 Cup vegetable stock or
1 cup of reserved liquor from boiled beans
1 Large onion finely chopped
2 Cloves garlic minced
1 tbsp olive oil
1 tbsp butter
1 tsp dried oregano
1 tsp **Tan Rosie's Garlic & Pepper Sauce (HOT)**
Sea salt and black pepper to taste

Ingredients For Sweet Potato Topping:

2lbs sweet potatoes
200g Grated mature cheddar cheese
1 tbsp butter
½ Cup double cream
100g grated mature cheese for sprinkling on top
Salt & black pepper to taste

Method For Black Bean Base:

1. In saucepan heat olive oil and butter over medium heat.
2. Add onions fry for 5 minutes until soft and golden brown.
3. Add garlic and oregano, stir and cook for further 1 minute.
4. Add Beans, stock/liquor, hot sauce and bring to the boil.
5. Turn heat down to low, cover pan and cook for 15 minutes.
6. Season to taste with salt and pepper.
7. In a baking dish, place bean mixture and allow to cool before adding sweet potato topping.

Method For Sweet Potato Topping:

1. Peel and boil sweet potato until tender in salted water.
2. Drain potato and mash, a potato ricer can be used which would give a smoother outcome
3. Add butter, cheese, double cream salt and pepper and blend thoroughly.
4. Place sweet potato topping on to black bean base and smoothed over.
5. Sprinkle over cheese
6. Bake in medium heat at gas mark 7 for 30 to 35 minutes until golden brown.

Vegetarian Dishes
Caribbean Style Nut Roast

This recipe is our twist on the humble nut roast, Caribbean style! It's perfect for Christmas lunch or for a special occasion with friends. We made this with an accompaniment of our own **Tan Rosie's Garlic & Pepper Sauce (HOT)**. It just gives an extra hit of heat which peps up the dish. Try it!

Serves 6

Ingredients:

150g Cashew nuts
150g Brazil nuts
250g Chestnuts
1 Cup fresh bread crumbs
1 Large onion chopped
2 Garlic cloves minced
½ Cup dried cranberries
1 tbsp Fresh thyme
1 tbsp Parsley chopped
2 Eggs beaten
1 Vegetable stock cube crushed
Pinch nutmeg
¼ tsp Allspice
1 tsp **Tan Rosie's Garlic & Pepper Sauce (HOT)**
¼ tsp sea salt
¼ teaspoon Black pepper
1 tbsp Olive oil
1 tbsp Butter

Method:

1. Grease loaf tin with butter.
2. Preheat oven to gas mark 7 or medium heat.
3. Place Brazil, cashew and chestnuts in food processor and coarsely ground.
4. Place nut mix in bowl.
5. Place oil and butter in frying pan on medium heat, add chopped onions and fry until golden brown, about 5 minutes.
6. Add garlic to onion and cook for 1 minute.
7. Remove from heat and cool.
8. Add cooled onion and garlic to nut mix and combine all other ingredients together.
9. Place nut roast in loaf tin, dot top of nut roast with butter.
10. Place nut roast in oven.
11. Bake for 40 to 45 minutes until top is golden brown.

Vegetarian Dishes
Caribbean Lime Butternut Squash & Cashew Stew
In a Coconut Sauce

This is a delicious way to use fresh limes in a comforting Caribbean Vegan stew. Perfect with white rice or cous cous. Add extra chilli for more of a kick

Serves 2/3

Ingredients:
1kg Butternut Squash, peeled & chipped into 1" pieces
150g Unsalted Cashew Nuts
1 Tin Coconut Milk
2 Tbsp **Tan Rosie Caribbean Lime Rub**
1 Lime, zest & juiced
Olive for frying & marinade
250ml Vegetable Stock
1 Red Chilli, deseeded & finely chopped
200g Spinach
1 Tsp Salt
1 Tsp Black Pepper
1 Tbsp Fresh Thyme

Method:
1. Place the chopped butternut squash into a bowl, drizzle some olive oil, add Caribbean Lime Rub, lime zest and juice. Massage through.
2. Place a saucepan onto a medium heat, add olive oil. Once heated, add marinated butternut squash and sauté for a few minutes.
3. Add spinach, then sauté for another minute. Add red chilli, salt, black pepper, vegetable stock, thyme and coconut milk. Bring to the boil, cover, reduce the heat to a simmer, then cook for 20 minutes or until butternut squash is softened.
4. Once cooked, remove from the heat, sprinkle a handful of cashew nuts over the top.
5. Serve with white rice. Delicious!

Tip:
Suitable for vegans.

Ital Stew

Ital stew is a famous Jamaican Rastafarian dish. "Ital" is taken from the word "vital." The Rastafarian diet is vegan, so eating pure and natural vegetables and pulses are essential to their religion. It's a colourful and hearty stew, perfect as a starter or main dish.

Serves 6

Ingredients:

1 Cup cooked kidney beans
1 Large onion chopped
4 Spring onions chopped
3 Cloves garlic minced
1 Cup sweet potato diced
1 Cup yam diced
1 Cup cassava diced
2 Large carrots diced
2 Sticks celery diced
1 Medium white potato diced
2 tbsp Olive oil
1 tbsp butter
½ Cup chopped tomato
4 Sprigs of thyme
4 Cups coconut milk
1 Cup vegetable stock
¼ tsp Allspice
¼ tsp Cinnamon
250g Spinach chopped
1 Scotch bonnet pepper
Salt and black pepper to taste
Pinch of saffron

Dumpling Ingredients:

1 Cup whole wheat flour
Pinch salt and black pepper
1 tsp sugar
Knob of butter or 1 Tbsp Olive Oil
Water to mix

Method:

1. Place olive oil and butter in saucepan and place on medium heat.
2. Place onions in saucepan and cook for 5 minutes until golden brown and soft.
3. Add garlic, cook for 1 minute.
4. Add carrots, celery and continue to cook for further 3 minutes
5. Add chopped tomato, allspice, cinnamon, saffron, thyme and scotch bonnet pepper, stir.
6. Add coconut milk, kidney beans, vegetable stock, bring to the boil cover pan and simmer for 15 minutes.
7. After 15 minutes, add vegetables, bring back to boil.
8. Add dumplings, continue cooking until vegetables are tender and dumplings are cooked.
9. Add spinach, spring onions and cook for further 5 minutes.

Dumplings Method:

1. Mix all ingredients together to firm stiff dough.
2. Leave to rest for 10 minutes.
3. Make small round balls.
4. Add to ital stew as directed above.

Macaroni Pie

Every Caribbean household eats macaroni pie! This is a staple dish in every home across all the islands. It's a comforting, delicious dish which we eat with anything from curry chicken, fried chicken and much more.

Serves 6

Ingredients:

200g Macaroni
1 Tsp Salt
400g Mature Cheddar
1 ½ Cups or 650ml Evaporated Milk, warmed
2 Eggs, beaten
1 Small Onion, minced
1 Clove Garlic, minced
50g Butter, softened
150g Breadcrumbs
½ Tsp English ground mustard powder
½ Tsp Grated Nutmeg
½ Tsp Ground Black Pepper
1 Level Tsp Smoked Paprika
1 Tbsp Olive Oil

Method:

1. Bring a saucepan with salted water to the boil.
2. Add macaroni to saucepan, stir and cook for 7 minutes – macaroni should be al dente.
3. Drain macaroni and return to saucepan.
4. Pre heat the oven to gas mark 7 or 220c.
5. In a mixing bowl and 300g of the cheddar cheese, beaten eggs, grated onions, evaporated milk, garlic, mustard, grated nutmeg, olive oil and ground black pepper, then whisk together.
6. Add the liquid mixture to macaroni and combine.
7. Grease a baking dish or foil tray with butter and pour in macaroni mixture.
8. Combine the remaining ingredients of the breadcrumbs, paprika and left over cheese into a topping for the pie.
9. Spread topping over pie and dot with butter.
10. Bake in oven for 30 to 35 minutes until topping is golden brown.
11. Remove from oven and allow to cool before cutting into it.

Tip:

This dish can be served as a main or side dish.

Side Dishes

Traditional Rice & Peas

Rice and peas is a very traditional dish in the Caribbean. Each region has its own twist on the recipe. Jamaicans tend to use kidney beans, but my family in Carriacou Grenada have always used pigeon peas or gungo peas. It's a timeless recipe that I hope you'll enjoy making.

Serves 4

Ingredients:
400g/ 1 Tin Gungo/Pigeon peas
400g Long Grain Rice
400ml/ 1 Tin Coconut Milk
1 tbsp Fresh thyme
1 Scotch bonnet pepper
1 Small Onion finely chopped
2 Garlic cloves minced
1 tbsp Olive oil
1 tbsp Butter
Salt and black pepper to taste
400ml Vegetable Stock

Method:
1. Place a frying pan on medium heat, add olive oil, butter and onions and sauté for 5 minutes.
2. Add garlic and thyme, fry for a further 1 minute.
3. Add coconut milk, vegetable stock, salt and black pepper and bring to the boil.
4. Add whole scotch bonnet pepper and gently stir.
5. Reduce heat to low and cover.
6. Allow to cook until all liquid is absorbed, and rice is tender for about 20/25 minutes.
7. Remove from heat and allow to rest covered for 10 minutes before serving. Remember to remove the scotch bonnet pepper!

Fried Plantains

Fried plantains are a superb side dish for any Caribbean meal. Make sure the plantains are ripe, as they will taste sweeter and juicer!

Serves 6

Ingredients:
4 Ripe plantains
Oil for frying
Salt and Black pepper

Method:
1. Peel plantains
2. Divide each plantain into 2 crossways, then each portion into 2 lengthways.
3. In frying pan, heat oil to medium hot.
4. Place plantains in hot oil, fry until golden brown on each side.
5. Remove from oil with slotted spoon, place onto absorbent kitchen paper.
6. Sprinkle with salt and pepper and serve.

Sweet Potato Mash

This is a great alternative to regular mash. You can serve this mash with a curry chicken, lamb or beef.

Serves 6

Ingredients:
1lb Sweet potato
1tbsp Butter
½ Cup double cream
1tsp Salt and pepper
2 Stalks spring onions finely chopped for garnish

Method:
1. Peel and cube sweet potato.
2. Place saucepan with water on heat. Add salt and sweet potato and bring to boil.
3. Reduce heat and simmer for 10 to 15 minutes.
4. Remove from heat and drain off water.
5. Return pan to heat for 1 minute to allow all water to evaporate.
6. Remove pan from heat, add butter, cream, salt and pepper to taste and mash all ingredients together to a smooth consistency.
7. A potato can be used to achieve this or a potato masher will do as well.
8. Serve with spring onion to garnish.

Tip:
White sweet potato is ideal for this mash. Available at any Asian supermarket/grocer.

Crushed Yams

This crushed yams recipe uses double cream to give a rich velvety taste. It tastes great with fish, or meat dishes with a rich sauce.

Serves 4

Ingredients:

1lb Yams
1tbsp Butter
1 tbsp Olive oil
1 tsp Salt
1 Large onion finely minced
1 Garlic clove minced
¼ Cup double cream
1 tbsp Chopped parsley

Method:

1. Peel yams and dice.
2. Place yams in saucepan with water and salt on heat. Bring to boil, reduce heat and simmer for 10 minutes or until yam is tender.
3. Remove from heat, drain water and discard. Cover yams and set aside.
4. Place oil and butter in a frying pan on medium heat.
5. Add onion, fry for 5 minutes, stirring until golden brown.
6. Add garlic and fry for a further 1 minute.
7. Add onion and garlic mixture to yam with double cream.
8. Crush mixture together.
9. Sprinkle with parsley and serve.

Coconut Rice

We served this coconut rice dish at our Bajan Supper Club night with a Beef stew. It's a popular side dish which can be eaten with a variety of main dishes.

Serves 6

Ingredients:
1 ½ Cups Basmati rice
2 Cups Coconut milk
1 Cup Vegetable stock
1 Medium onion minced
1 tbsp Olive oil
1 tbsp Butter
1 tsp salt
Black pepper
Chopped parsley for garnish

Method:
1. Soak basmati rice in cold water for 30 minutes, then drain.
2. In saucepan, add oil and butter and place on medium heat, fry onions for 5 minutes, stirring occasionally until golden brown.
3. Add drained rice to onions, stirring to allow rice to be covered with the mixture.
4. Add vegetable stock, coconut milk, salt and pepper to taste, stir, bring to boil.
5. Cover pan, reduce heat to simmer, cook for 10 minutes until liquid is absorbed.
6. Turn off heat and leave covered for another 15 minutes.
7. Garnish with parsley and serve.

Tip:
Any left over rice can used in a stir fry the next day.

Baked Plantains in Orange Juice

This is one of my favourite recipes for plantains. At our supper club, I like to experiment with traditional Caribbean ingredients and this side dish is a crowd pleaser!

Serves 8

Ingredients:
4 Ripe plantains
Rind and juice of 1 orange
Salt and pepper to taste
1 tbsp Butter
1 tbsp Chopped spring onions

Method:
1. Grease baking dish with some butter.
2. Preheat oven to medium heat gas mark 7.
3. Peel plantains, cut each into 2 crossways and each portion into 2 lengthways.
4. Arrange sliced plantains in greased dish, sprinkle with rind of orange and juice, salt and pepper and dot with butter.
5. Cover with foil securely and bake in oven for 25 to 30 minutes.
6. Remove from oven sprinkle with spring onions and serve.

Roasted Sweet Potatoes

This is a really easy recipe to try if you want roast potatoes with a twist!

Serves 6

Ingredients:
2 lbs Sweet potato, peeled and cut into chunks
3 Shallots sliced thickly
2 Cloves garlic sliced
3 Sprigs of fresh thyme
2 tbsp olive oil
1 tbsp butter
1 tsp Sea salt
Black pepper

Method:
1. Preheat oven to gas mark 7.
2. Place all ingredients into a large freezer bag, seal and mix together.
3. Empty ingredients from freezer bag into roasting tin, discard freezer bag.
4. Place in roasting tin. Roast for 45 minutes until golden brown, turning occasionally.
5. Remove from oven, discard thyme sprigs and serve while hot.

Side Dishes

Plantain Dumplings

I came up with this recipe to use leftover ripe plantains. It tastes fantastic combined with a dumpling mixture. You can add these dumplings to stews or eat them as a side dish. Enjoy them!

Serves 8

Ingredients:
1 Very ripe plantain, peeled and mashed
1 Cup self raising flour
½ tsp Salt
½ tsp black pepper
1 Knob of butter
Water to mix
Olive oil for garnish

Method:
1. Place all ingredients in a mixing bowl.
2. Mix thoroughly.
3. Add some water and mix to form firm dough.
4. Cover and allow to rest for 15 minutes.
5. In a saucepan water and bring to boil on medium heat.
6. Roll out dough into small balls and drop into the boiling salted water, cover and boil on reduced heat for 10 minutes or until dumplings are cooked through.
7. When cooked, the dumplings will rise to the top of the liquid.
8. Remove dumplings from pan, sprinkle with olive oil and serve.

Side Dishes
Plantain Mash

Another great way to use plantain is to mash it! It's so easy to do and tastes amazing.

Serves 4

Ingredients:
4 Ripe/Yellow Plantains
3 Spring Onions, thinly chopped
1 Garlic Clove, thinly chopped
1 Tbsp Fresh Thyme
½ Tsp Sea Salt
½ Tsp Black Pepper
Olive Oil
Butter (optional)

Method:
1. Peel the plantains, slice into 2' pieces and either steam them for about 10 minutes or until cooked.
2. When the plantain is cooked, transfer to a bowl and mash with a fork to desired consistency.
3. Add some olive oil to a saucepan and sauté spring onions for 1 minute on a medium heat. Add the garlic, thyme, salt and pepper and stir for a minute.
4. Turn the heat off the saucepan and add your mashed plantain with a drop of extra olive oil and a knob of butter, then mix through.
5. Serve with jerk chicken or any other main dish. Enjoy!

Desserts

Farine Biscuits

Farine, also known as Garri, is made from cassava. Cassava is a root vegetable that can be milled to make flour or treated like a potato. It's very common in tropical countries including the Caribbean. You can use the flour for sweet or savoury recipes. These sweet biscuits are a delight! **Makes 24**

Ingredients:

1 cup or 250g Farine
1 cup or 250g All-purpose flour
1/2 Cup or 125g sugar
150g butter
1 egg, beaten
1 tsp baking powder
1 tsp salt
1 tsp cinnamon
1/4 tsp grated nutmeg
milk for combining
Baking tray
Baking Parchment Paper

Method:

1 Preheat oven to gas mark 6
2. In a mixing bowl, combine all dry ingredients.
3. Rub in the butter in dry ingredients.
4. Add beaten egg and 1/2 cup of milk and mix to form a firm dough.
5. If is dry add more milk and combine.
6. On a floured surface, roll out dough into ½ centimetre thickness.
7. Using a cookie cutter or a glass, cut out your biscuits.
8. On a baking tray layer baking parchment.
9. Place your biscuits onto baking tray
10. With a fork, prick biscuits all over, this allows for even baking.
11. Bake in oven at gas mark 6 for 20 minutes or until golden brown and firm.

Desserts
Nutmeg Ice Cream

Nutmeg is one of our favourite spices we use a lot of in Carriacou, Grenada. Adding it to ice cream only makes it more yummy in this sumptuous recipe!

Serves 8

Ingredients:
500ml Ready-made custard (really good quality one)
350 ml Double cream
1 Tin Condensed milk
1 tsp Vanilla extract
1 tbsp Freshly ground nutmeg
Pinch of salt

Method:
1. In mixing bowl, place all ingredients and blend using a hand held whisk.
2. Whisk until thickened.
3. Place mixture into lidded plastic container and freeze.
4. An ice cream maker can be used, follow manufacturer's instructions.

Mango & Mint Sorbet

If you want a refreshing dessert, then this is the recipe for you. (It's also great for your breath too!)

Serves 6

Ingredients:
4 Ripe mangos peeled, stoned and chopped
3 tbsp Fresh mint chopped
300g Icing sugar
Juice of 3 limes
2 tbsp Rosewater

Method:
1. Place all ingredients into a food processer, blend to a pureed stage.
2. Remove from blender and churn in an ice cream maker according to manufacturer's instructions.
3. Transfer to a lidded container and store in freezer until ready to serve.

Tip:
Can be placed into a container after blending in food processor and freeze, then forking or whisking after 2 to 3 hours on 2 occasions.

Coconut & Blueberry Muffins

These yummy muffins are great for breakfast or for an afternoon treat. It's a quick and easy recipe that the whole family will enjoy.

Makes 12

Ingredients:

100g Unsalted Butter, softened
1 Tbsp Butter melted, for greasing
50g Desiccated Coconut
140g Caster Sugar
2 Eggs, large
200g Coconut Milk
1 Tsp Vanilla Extract
4 Tbsp Milk
250g Plain Flour
2 tsp Baking Powder
1 tsp Bicarbonate of soda
125g Blueberries

Method:

1. Preheat the oven to 180/200oC or gas mark 6/7.
2. Using a 12-hole muffin tray, line it with paper cases.
3. Mix the butter and sugar together into a smooth paste.
4. Add the eggs and mix well until it's smooth.
5. Stir in the milk, coconut milk and vanilla extract.
6. Add the flour, bicarbonate of soda, baking powder and a pinch of salt into the bowl and mix through.
7. Add the coconut and blueberries, mix through and fill your muffin cases.
8. Place in the oven and bake for 5 mins, then reduce the heat to 160/180oC or gas mark 4 and bake for another 15/20 minutes until it's golden brown and risen. Use a cocktail stick and insert into the centre, if it comes out clean, then it's cooked.
9. Turn out onto a wire rack and cool.

Tip:

Frozen berries can be used.

Plantain & Pumpkin Ice Cream

This is truly a unique Caribbean flavour combo! The humble ice cream is transformed using two of the most popular ingredients in the Caribbean. It's delicious and must be tasted to be believed!

Serves 10

Ingredients

2 Ripe Plantains steamed, pureed and cooled
250g Pumpkin steamed, pureed and cooled
1 Tin Condensed Milk
250ml Double Cream
250ml Good quality ready-made Custard
1 Tsp grated nutmeg
1 Tsp grated cinnamon
2 Tsp Vanilla Extract
1 Tbs Honey

Method:

1. Combine all ingredients in a mixing bowl and using an electric whisk, whip until blended and thickened to a soft peak consistency.
2. A KitchenAid machine or an ice cream maker can be used.
3. Transfer to a lidded container and freeze.

Once frozen enjoy!

Desserts
Tan Rosie's Ginger Cake

This is another firm favourite from our Supper Club events. The ginger syrup makes a big difference to the cake, giving it extra moisture and yumminess! It tastes great with ice cream or vanilla cream too!

Serves 8

Ingredients:
250g Butter
6 eggs, Lightly beaten
4 tbsp Grated root ginger
1 tsp Vanilla extract
200 ml Milk
2 tsp Baking powder
320g Plain flour
4 tsp Ground ginger
1 ½ tsp Ground cinnamon
½ tsp Salt
275g Soft dark brown sugar
2 Pieces stem ginger sliced thinly
100 ml Sugar syrup (syrup from stem ginger can be used)

Method:
1. Preheat oven to gas mark 6
2. Grease 9" cake tin
3. In mixing bowl, cream together butter and sugar.
4. Add beaten eggs, continue to mix well, add milk, vanilla extract and grated ginger and mix.
5. Mix all dry ingredients together and add to the butter mixture and fold in.
6. Pour batter into greased cake tin.
7. Place in oven and bake for 60 minutes or until when skewer is inserted it comes out clean when removed. If after 60 minutes, it's still not cooked, put it back in for a further 15 minutes until cooked.
8. Remove from over, decorate with sliced stem ginger, drizzle over ginger syrup and allow to cool.

Guava & Apple Crumble

Adding a Caribbean fruit to a traditional English dessert can really transform your dish! Guava tastes perfect next to apples. Expect very clean bowls afterwards!

Serves 10

Ingredients:

2 Cups Guava, de seeded and chopped
2 Cups Apples chopped
½ tsp Ground cinnamon
¼ Cup Sugar

For Crumble topping

1 Cup Flour
1 Cup Oats
250g Butter
½ tsp Salt
½ Cup Sugar
½ tsp Ground cinnamon

Method:

1. Preheat oven to gas mark 7
2. Grease dish
3. In mixing bowl, add guava, apples, cinnamon and sugar, mix together.
4. Pour fruit mixture into dish and set aside.
5. To make crumble, place flour salt and butter into mixing bowl, rub in mixture to fine bread crumbs.
6. Add sugar, oats and cinnamon and mix well together.
7. Spread crumble mixture over fruit mixture.
8. Bake in oven for 50 minutes.
9. Remove from oven.
10. Serve with cream or custard

Bolo Boracho
(Tipsy Rum Cake)

This is another fab Cuban recipe that we served up for very happy guests! The rum syrup is very important to add extra flavour and moistness to the cake.

Serves 8

Ingredients:
3 Cups Plain flour
3 tsp Baking powder
1 ½ Cups Softened butter
1 Cup Heavy cream
5 eggs Lightly beaten
1 ½ Cups Light brown sugar
Zest of 1 Lemon or lime
1 Cup Dark rum
2 tsp Vanilla extract
½ tsp Ground cinnamon
½ tsp Ground nutmeg
¼ tsp Salt

For rum syrup:
1 Cup Sugar
½ Cup Water
¾ Cup Dark rum
¼ Cup Butter

Method:
1. Preheat oven to gas mark 6
2. Grease 10" cake tin
3. In mixing bowl, cream together butter and sugar.
4. Add beaten eggs and mix well.
5. Add heavy cream, rum and zest of lemon and mix.
6. Mix all dry ingredients together and fold into batter mixture.
7. Pour batter into cake tin. Bake in oven at gas mark 6 for 60 minutes or until when skewer is inserted in cake and removed clean.
8. Remove from oven and leave in cake tin to cool.

To make rum syrup:
1. Place saucepan on hob on medium heat.
2. To saucepan add water and sugar.
3. Bring to the boil, reduce heat and simmer for 5 minutes until sugar is melted.
4. Remove from heat, add butter and whisk, add rum and continue to whisk until blended.
5. With a skewer make some holes in cake and pour over rum syrup.
6. Leave for at least 3 days until flavours develop.

Tip:
Some extra rum can be spooned over cake for a more tipsy cake.

Desserts
Coconut & Banana Pancakes
with a Sticky Rum Sauce

This is a great way to use Caribbean ingredients to transform the humble pancake. The sticky rum sauce adds a luxury twist to this sweet treat.

Serves 4

Ingredients for Pancake:
1 Cup or 250g Plain Flour
1 Tbsp White Sugar
2 Tsp Baking Powder
¼ Tsp Salt
1 Egg, beaten
1 Cup or 250ml Coconut Milk
2 Ripe Bananas, mashed
¼ Tsp Nutmeg

Ingredients for Rum Sauce:
½ Cup or 125g Dark Brown Sugar
¼ Cup or 60ml Dark Rum
2 Tbsp Butter
1 Tsp Molasses

Pancake Method:
1. Combine flour, white sugar, baking powder, coconut milk, nutmeg, egg and salt into a bowl and stir. Add mashed banana and continue to stir. The batter will be slightly lumpy.
2. Heat a lightly oiled frying pan over a medium/high heat. (A non-stick frying pan is better).
3. Pour or scoop the batter onto the frying pan and cook until golden brown on each side.

Sauce Method:
1. Melt the butter and sugar in a saucepan.
2. Add the rest of the ingredients and bring to the boil.
3. Reduce the heat and simmer, stirring occasionally or for 3.4 minutes until the sugar has dissolved and the mixture is thickened and bubbly.
4. Drizzle over pancakes and serve.

Drinks

Rum Punch

Fond memories of sitting on Paradise beach in Carriacou Grenada come flooding back whilst drinking this rum punch! If you are in Carriacou, try using the local Jack Iron Rum instead of regular white rum, but be careful - it's very potent!

Ingredients:
3 Cups White rum
3 Cups Pineapple juice
3 Cups Orange juice
2 Cups Sugar syrup
¼ Cup Grenadine
¼ tsp Nutmeg
1 tsp Angostura bitters
Ice cubes

Method:
1. Place all ingredients into large jug and stir.
2. Serve with a sprinkling of nutmeg on top.

Monica's Ginger Drink

We normally serve my ginger drink as a complimentary drink for our Supper Club guests. After one glass, people generally want to drink the whole jug, so be warned - make more!

Ingredients:
8oz Fresh ginger peeled and chopped
2 Cups Sugar
3 litres Water
Juice and zest of 3 lemons
1 Stick cinnamon
1 tsp Angostura bitters
Ice cubes to serve

Method:
1. Place ginger with 1 litre of water in blender and puree.
2. Transfer to large saucepan; add rest of water, sugar, cinnamon and zest of lemon.
3. Bring to the boil over medium heat.
4. Reduce heat and simmer for 10 to 15 minutes.
5. Remove from heat, add lemon juice and Angostura bitters, stir.
6. Cover saucepan and let ginger develop.
7. When cold, strain using muslin cloth or fine sieve.
8. Serve with ice cubes.

Drinks
Sorrel

Sorrel is a popular drink in the Caribbean made from the petals of the sorrel tree. You can buy them dried from Asian supermarkets and some larger supermarkets too. If you want an extra kick, add some rum!

Ingredients:
2 Cups Dried sorrel petals
4 Cups Sugar
3 litres Water
1 Stick cinnamon
3 Whole clove
2" Piece fresh ginger, sliced thinly

Method:
1. In large saucepan place all ingredients and bring to the boil stirring until sugar is dissolved.
2. Reduce heat and simmer for 15 minutes.
3. Turn off heat after 15 minutes and allow to cool
4. Strain using sieve or muslin cloth.
5. Pour into sterilised bottles and refrigerate.
6. Serve with ice cubes when ready.

Virgin Soursop Cocktail

Soursop is a delicately sweet and succulent fruit, grown in many tropical countries. It makes a refreshing virgin cocktail for summer bbq's.

Serves 4

Ingredients:
2 Soursops or 2 Tins
Soursop Juice
1 Tsp Angostura
Bitters
Nutmeg
Ice
Mint

Method:
1. In a tall jug add ice
2. Then add soursop juice, Angostura and stir.
3. Pour the juice into a cocktail glass, grate a little nutmeg to garnish and a slice of lime.
4. Enjoy!

Supper Club Menus

Grenada

Grenada is a part of the Windward Islands in the Caribbean. Grenada is affectionately known as 'The Spice Island' due to the abundance of nutmeg and mace that is grown on its shores. It's one of the largest exporters of this precious spice which can be used in cooking or for medicinal purposes.

Grenadian food is a mixture of African, Indian and native Caribbean cuisine, to name a few. Due to the climate, alot of the meat and fish are 'corned' or salted to preserve them. Salted meat and fish are used in various Grenadian dishes.

Limes are one of the citrus fruits that are grown in Grenada and it's other parishes such as as Carriacou. They are used to clean meat and fish and they are added to juices and many other dishes.

Grenada's national dish is Oildown (page 41) which is a stew consiting of dumplings, salted meats, callaloo, breadfruit, chicken and other vegetables. It's then cooked in coconut milk with other spices such as nutmeg and allspice.

The menu overleaf is a mixture of some traditional dishes along with our own interpretations. We hope you'll enjoy trying them!

Caribbean Supper Club
Come & Dine In Our Living Room!

Grenadian Kitchen

Appetizer

**Corn Fritters & Sweet Potato Fritters
with a Spicy Lime Sauce**
&
Complimentary Grenadian Rum Punch Cocktail

Starter

**Salt Fish on a bed of Coo Coo (Polenta)
&
Traditional Home Baked Bread**

Main

**Traditional Rice & Peas (Pigeon Peas) with Curry Mutton
or
Channa Dhal (Chick Pea & Potato Curry) with plain rice**

Side dishes: Steamed Broccoli, Carrots & Fried Plantain

Dessert

**Pumpkin Pie with Fresh Cream
or
Nutmeg Ice Cream**

Shhhh... It's A Secret!

Trinidad

Trinidad is a part of the Leeward Islands in the Caribbean. It's smaller sister island is Tobago.

Trinidad cuisine contains a vast array of culinary influences from Africa, India, China, Portugal and native Caribbean. Trinidad has many popular dishes such as 'Doubles, ' Shark & Bake' and 'Macaronie Pie' (page 64).

The Indian influence on Trinidads' cusine is very strong. Trinidadians love their curries, rotis and dhals. There are a variety of different rotis from Trinidad that taste fantastic. Our favourite is 'Paratha Roti' or 'Buss Up Shut' (page 50). This particular roti consists of layers which is then torn up and pulled apart and served with a curry with plently of sauce.

We've included a few traditional Trinidadian recipes in our menu overleaf, but there are so many more fantastic recipes out there to try also - hopefully these will give you a head start!

Enjoy cooking!

Caribbean Supper Club
Trinidadian Kitchen

Appetizer

Phoulourie & Accras (Fritters)
served with
Spicy Banana Chutney & Tamarind Sauce

Complimentary Homemade Ginger Beer

Starter

Stuffed Plantains with Spinach

Main

Geera Pork with Buss-Up-Shut (Roti)
OR
Spicy Aubergine & Sweet Potato Bake

SIDE DISHES:
Macaroni Pie
Steamed Green Beans & Carrots

Dessert

Mango & Mint Sorbet
OR
Tan Rosie's Ginger Cake with Fresh Cream

Shhhh... It's A Secret!

Cuba

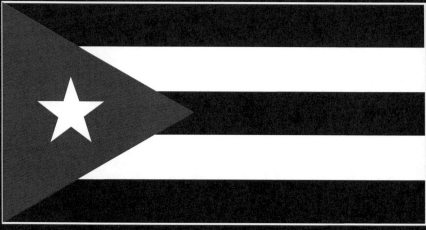

Cuba is a Spanish speaking island and it's one of the largest in the Caribbean.

Cuba's main culinary influence is Spanish and African. Ingredients such as rum, black beans and olives are used in a variety of dishes.

Cuban cusine is very simple. Cubans don't usually use alot of chillies in their food. As with other Caribbean islands, they use alot of root vegetables such as yucca and sweet potatoes.

Stews and soups are very common. These are normally eaten with rice or on their own.

Cuban sandwiches are a popular lunchtime meal utilising meats, poultry, cuban bread and cheeses.

The base of most sauces and stews is called 'Sofrito.' This is a sauce consisting of garlic, onions and tomatoes it can be added to almost any dish.

The most popular sauce is called 'Mojo' (page 22). This is a sauce made from oil, garlic, onion and other spices. It can be combined with other fruits such as mango to create some great tasting sauces.

Have a look at the menu overleaf for some great ideas for your Cuban menu!

Cuban Kitchen

Appetizer

Mariquitas de Plátanos
(Plantain Crisps) with Salsa dip

Starter

Pure de Calabaza
(Creamy Pumpkin Soup)

Main

Pollo Borracho with Arroz Amarillo
(Drunken Chicken with Yellow Rice)

OR

Frijoles Negros & Bonito Bake
(Black Bean & Sweet Potato Bake)

Side Dishes: Steamed Brocolli & Carrots

Dessert

Monica's Cuban Rum Cake
with Cream or Custard

Shhhh... It's A Secret!

Jamaica

Jamaica is located in the northern part of the Caribbean and takes culinary influences from the native Caribbeans, Africa, Spanish and Chinese to name but a few.

Many of you will be familiar with some Jamaican dishes which include, Jerk Chicken (page 52) and Ackee & Salt Fish (page 32). Other popular dishes include Escoveitch fish which is made with lime juice, Fish Tea (soup) the list goes on!

Jerk is a very poplar marinade and style of cooking in Jamaica. Meat is marinaded with a wet sauce or dry seasoning rub. It is traditionally cooked on large open fires using particular varieties of wood which helps to give the meats a very unique flavour. More recently oil drums are converted into barbecues which are used by street stalls and during carnival to roast the various jerk pork and chicken dishes.

We've combined a selection of traditional Jamaican dishes with our own variations.

Have a go at the menu!

Caribbean Supper Club

Jamaican Kitchen
Appetizer
Sweet Potato Crisps with Sweet Lime Sauce

Starter
Ackee & Salt Fish with Fried Dumplings

Main
Curry Goat with Rice & Peas
OR
Ital Stew with Rice (veg)

Side Dishes: Steamed Green Beans & Carrots

Dessert
Ginger Cake with Cream or Custard
OR
Jamaican Rum & Raisin Ice Cream

 Shhhh... It's A Secret!

Barbados

Barbados is a very popular English speaking island in the Caribbean.

Typical Caribbean dishes such as 'Cou Cou' (polenta) and 'Salt Fish' are cooked slightly differently with additional ingredients. Barbadian or 'Bajan' Cou Cou is made with okras which gives the dish a very different twist compared to the other Caribbean recipes.

Flying Fish and Cou Cou is a Bajan national dish which is eaten by the locals especially on national holidays. Their main source of protein is fish including, shark, tuna, flying fish, snapper and king fish. Bajan's enjoy a variety of different 'salted' fish along with many other Caribbean islands.

Bajan's love their desserts such peanut brittle, tamarind balls (tamarind is a fruit) and coconut bread.

Bajan's use a wide variety of fruit and vegetables in their cooking including: plantains, breadfruit, okras, christphene (a sugarless fruit), limes and cassava. They love their hot sauces of which they use in a variety of dishes!

Enjoy trying our Bajan menu ideas!
114.

Tan Rosie

Caribbean Supper Club

Come & Dine In Our Living Room!

Bajan Kitchen

Appetizer

*Cassava Crisps with
Pineapple & Mint Sauce*

Starter

*Cou Cou (polenta) with
Fried Red Snapper*

Main

Bajan Beef Stew with Coconut Rice

OR

Macaroni Pie with Spiced Tomato Sauce

Side Dishes: **Steamed Brocolli & Carrots**

Dessert

Guava & Apple Crumble
with Cream or Custard

OR

Fresh Tropical Fruit Salad

Shhhh... It's A Secret!

Aruba

Aruba is located in the southwestern part of the Caribbean and is a part of the Dutch Leeward Islands. Aruba is very close to Curacao and Bonaire.

Aruba takes it's culinary influences from the Dutch, Spain, Africa and native Caribbean people.

Arubans eat alot of stews, soups and fish such as Shrimps, Calamari, Shark, Swordfish and Conch.

Popular Aruban dishes include: Balchi di Pisca (salt cod balls page 29), Cala (bean fritters), Stoba (goat stew), Sopa di Pompuna (a pumpkin dish) and Keri Keri (a popular dish made from green peppers, fish, celery, onions and basil leaves).

We hope you enjoy trying our Aruban influence menu. You can easily swap out any ingredients to suit your taste when trying these recipes. Good luck and enjoy!

Tan Rosie

Caribbean Supper Club
Come & Dine In Our Living Room!

Aruban Kitchen

Appetizer
Yucca, Plantain & Sweet Potato Crisps
with Mango Mojo Sauce & Chilli Lime Sauce
Complimentary Virgin Sorrel Drink
Starter
Balchi di Pisca
(Salt Cod Balls) with Tamarind Sauce
& Homemade Bread and Side Salad
Main
Spicy Slow Roast Leg of Mutton
OR Veg. Option
Caribbean Style Nut Roast
with Onion Gravy
Side Dishes: Rice & Peas, Roasted Sweet Potato
Steamed Vegetables
Dessert
Bolo Boracho
(Tipsy Rum Cake) with Cream or Custard
OR
Caribbean Fruit Platter

Shhhh... It's A Secret!

Weights & Measurements

Gas Mark	Fahrenheit	Celsius	Description
1/4	225	110	Very cool/very slow
1/2	250	130	---
1	275	140	cool
2	300	150	---
3	325	170	---
4	350	180	---
5	375	190	---
6	400	200	moderate
7	425	220	hot
8	450	230	---
9	475	240	very hot

1 tablespoon (tbsp) =	3 teaspoons (tsp)
1/16 cup =	1 tablespoon
1/8 cup =	2 tablespoons
1/6 cup =	2 tablespoons + 2 teaspoons
1/4 cup =	4 tablespoons
1/3 cup =	5 tablespoons + 1 teaspoon
3/8 cup =	6 tablespoons
1/2 cup =	8 tablespoons
2/3 cup =	10 tablespoons + 2 teaspoons
3/4 cup =	12 tablespoons
1 cup =	150gm
8 fluid ounces (fl oz) =	1 cup
1 pint (pt) =	2 cups
1 quart (qt) =	2 pints
4 cups =	1 quart
1 gallon (gal) =	4 quarts
16 ounces (oz) =	1 pound (lb)
1 milliliter (ml) =	1 cubic centimeter (cc)
1 inch (in) =	2.54 centimeters (cm)

Capacity		Weight	
1/5 teaspoon	1 milliliter	1 oz	28 grams
1 teaspoon	5 ml	1 pound	454 grams
1 tablespoon	15 ml		
1 fluid oz	30 ml		
1/5 cup	47 ml		
1 cup 237 ml			
2 cups (1 pint)	473 ml		
4 cups (1 quart)	.95 liter		
4 quarts (1 gal.)	3.8 liters		

Index

Index

Index